Table of Contents

1. Volvo & Terrafugia Link Up on Flying Cars
2. Commercial Supersonic Flights
3. Solar Cars To Go Mass Market
4. Trains With No Wheels, No Engines, No Pollution
5. Virgin Hyperloop One
6. Larry Page's Flying Car and Boat
7. "Classiest" Flying Car
8. Boeing's Hypersonic Passenger Jet
9. Flying Motorcycles
10. Jaguar's Electric Boat
11. Where's Your Jet Pack?
12. Electric Passenger Planes
13. China's Hypersonic Jet
14. Solar Drone Aircraft Powered by Laser Beams
15. Electric Motorcycles to Debut in 2019
16. DARPA's Truck Wheels That Change in Motion
17. Google's Self-Driving Car
18. DARPA's Hypersonic Aircraft
19. Virgin Galactic Readies for Takeoff
20. Smart Cars on Smart Roads
21. Next Generation Flying by Hexacopter
22. Ingenious Flying Car
23. Flying Car-Off Road Vehicle
24. Populist Personal Flying
25. Dutch Personal Flying Machine
26. MIT's Drone Boat
27. Easy to Fly Personal Flying Machine
28. Japan's Personal Flying Machine
29. British Personal Flying Machine
30. Georgia Tech's Flying Car

31. NASA's Unmanned Aircraft
32. Not Your Average Flying Machine
33. Where's the US in the Bullet Train Race?
34. NASA's Supersonic Passenger Jet
35. Hyperloop Gets Real
36. Dutch Flying Car
37. Your Flying Taxi is Here
38. USAF Secret Space Ship
39. DARPA's Robot Ship
40. Electric Powered Planes
41. DARPA's Flying Truck
42. DARPA's Space Plane
43. Orbiting Space Hotels
44. Flying, Driving Drones
45. Charged Roads for Electric Cars
46. Helicopter Cars
47. Terrafugia's TF-2
48. Tiny Robots With Application for Drones
49. Elon Musk's Loop Lift
50. High Tech Champagne in Space
51. World 1st, No Emissions Hydrogen Train
52. Exploring Mars

Author's Biography

Ed Kane created and serves as Executive Producer of CEO Global Foresight. CGF is a national program on PBS focused on breakthrough innovation changing our lives for the better. Guests have included the CEO's of Bayer AG, DARPA (the US Defense Department's Advanced Research Projects Agency), Terrafugia which created the world's first flying car and Adidas AG.

He also created and served as Executive Producer of CEO Corner originally for Bloomberg Radio. It was an hour interview program with the world's most innovative and entrepreneurial CEO's. Ed moved the program to television. It has aired on New England Cable News (NECN) for fifteen years. Guests have included the CEO's of Comcast, P&G, ExxonMobil and Verizon.

Ed is a science graduate of the University of Pennsylvania. He is an avid researcher into the future of breakthrough innovation and its impact on humanity.

Introduction

Of the thousands of reports and television shows we've done as journalists, by far the most interesting were innovations that will change our future. A hypersonic jet, flying at 7673 mph, that can take you from New York to Tokyo in one hour & 23 minutes; a hyperloop train, travelling 760 mph, that can take you from Los Angeles to San Francisco, 350 miles in 35 minutes; a flying car like the TFX that allows you to take-off from your driveway and land at your mall parking lot avoiding all traffic. Because of our innovators, we have a fascinating future.

This book "Important Innovations" is a collection of fascinating innovation. Volume One: Transportation seeks to bring to light the fascinating travel innovations that will be impacting our future. Some in a year or two, others in a decade or two or three.

These brief reports are fun reads, enlightening and great for conversation.

We hope you will enjoy reading them as much as we enjoyed researching them, meeting many of the innovators and writing the reports.

Many thanks to the innovators who work tirelessly to change our lives for the better! And thanks and best to you Reader.

Maryanne Kane and Ed Kane

1. Volvo & Terrafugia Link-Up on Flying Cars

Terrafugia's TFX Concept Flying Car

Changing Your Commute Forever

Volvo and Terrafugia have the same parent company, Geely Automotive Group of China. Thanks to Geely, the intersection of MIT engineering at Terrafugia, Swedish automotive expertise and a lot of cash from China is supercharging production of the world's 1st FAA and NTSB approved flying car. Volvo hopes to make it available for you to buy in 2019.

The Transition and TFX

US-based Terrafugia, started by MIT Ph.D engineers, has been developing flying cars for the past decade. They have The

Transition, a flying and driving car/plane and a prototype the TFX with vertical takeoff and landing like a helicopter, that also drives. The Transition can travel speeds up to 200 mph, has fold out wings, dual electric motors and a range of 400 miles on a charge. The Transition seats 2 and will go to market first at a provisional price of $235,000.

Lots of Competition in Crowded, Flying Car Skies

Uber and NASA have combined forces and will be launching their flying car in 2023. They claim it will cut commuting times by more than half. There are a lot more flying car players globally. It looks like the future of transportation is flying and driving right to your door.

2. Commercial Supersonic Flights

Artist Rendering: Courtesy of Boom Technology

Sir Richard Branson & Boom

The age of supersonic passenger travel is coming very soon, if Virgin's Sir Richard Branson has his way. He's heavily investing and banking on it. American startup Boom Technology, which Branson is bankrolling, is developing a Mach 2.2 supersonic passenger jet. That converts into approximately 1,676 mph or 27.94 miles per minute. Its Baby Boom XB1 demonstrator jet will be tested in 2019 to validate key technologies for commercial flights. XB1 is a 2 seater. Boom already has the Baby Boom engines in the hanger and is currently building the wings and tail. The supersonic commercial jet, carrying 55 passengers, will debut in 2023. Five airlines, including Virgin, have ordered 76 jets. Boom is getting ready for takeoff.

Arrive In Half The Time

As you can see in the artist's rendering, Boom resembles the Concorde. It's an evolutionary design with a lot of extra lift. It has a range of 4500 nautical miles. At Mach 2.2, it's two and a half times faster than commercial jets. Boom is 10% faster than the Concorde. The Concorde hasn't flown in 15 years. It was riddled by high operating costs, poor fuel mileage and low passenger bookings. In Boom, the sonic boom generated in flight is greatly reduced. The boom is 30 times less than that of the Concorde. Boom will cruise at 60,000 feet.

Big Time Saver

Who wouldn't love it. New York to London is 3:15 hours. That's half the current time of 7 hours. You could actually make it a getaway for a day. Roundtrip price-tag is $5000, the equivalent of today's business class. Or, LA to Sydney in 6:45 hours - half the time. Japan Airlines and Branson's space travel company Virgin Galactic will operate Boom supersonic jets for Branson. Branson believes supersonic flights will fit well into 500 global markets.

Crowded Skies

Supersonic jets are well under development. Besides Branson and Boom Technology, a number of other global entities are building them including NASA.

3. Solar Cars To Go Mass Market

Photo: Hanergy Solar Car

Hanergy's Solar Electric Cars

Is this the dawn of solar powered cars for consumers? Some experts believe the future of the automotive industry is solar. It's green driving with zero emissions - no CO_2
Solar cars are typically electric vehicles powered solely or mainly by solar energy. Photovoltaic cells contained in the solar panels convert the sun's energy into electricity. They combine some of the technologies used in the aerospace, alternative energy, automotive and bicycle industries. The design of the cars has been limited by the amount of solar panels needed to draw in enough solar energy to power the vehicles. As a result, prototype solar cars have primarily been built for solar car racing. But now that is changing.

Road Ready

Chinese solar panel manufacturer Hanergy has developed four prototype solar cars for the consumer mass market. Production is scheduled for next year. The cars are equipped with lithium ion batteries powered by the sun. They'll first be offered to Chinese consumers and are styled like a normal car.

Sun Power

Hanergy says exposure to 5 to 6 hours of sunlight enable the cars to travel 50 miles on solar power alone. The maximum range of the vehicle is 217 miles. According to the company, the current solar energy conversion rate is 32%. They project 38% by 2020, 42% by 2025, making a fully solar powered car possible.

4. Trains With No Wheels, No Engine,, No Pollution

Maglev Train

So Why Aren't They at a Train Station Near You?

They're green, clean, fast and quiet. No wheels, one track. Maglev stands for magnetic levitation. They glide on a cushion of air. Because of the way Maglev works, there's now little chance of derailment. The higher the train gets from the track, the stronger the magnetic force pushing it back. It's a greener transit solution. One problem - they're very expensive.

Magnetic Levitation Travel

The tech uses magnetic fields to lift the train a small distance above the track and make it move. It's much faster than a regular train. A Maglev in Japan just broke a world record at 600 mph. A trip from Toronto to Vancouver is forecast to take 3 hours on Maglev by 2035.

All Aboard in Asia

Only a handful of commercially viable systems have been built. Only 3 survive - all in Asia. China likes the system so much it plans to launch it in 12 cities by 2020. It has the world's fastest operational system at 268 mph. South Korea has an unmanned system called Ecobee. And Japan is building a system that just tested at speeds of 600mph.

Why Not More Systems

The drag is money. In the US, it would cost an estimated $100 million per mile to build and there's no guarantee of a profit. For now, Asia is the magnetic force in railway.

5. Virgin Hyperloop One

Source: Virgin – CEO Sir Richard Branson

Proof of Concept and Tested

Virgin Hyperloop One is among a number of businesses developing hyperloop systems. The hyperloop is a revolutionary technology that will dramatically cut travel times between cities. Virgin Hyperloop One has a lot of money behind it - $295 million from Sir Richard Branson's Virgin, GE Ventures and SNCF. The company has already built a proof of concept vehicle. It's been successfully tested. The "pod" levitated, accelerated, glides, braked and came to a stop. The company continues to move the technology forward.

Levitation and Gliding

Virgin Hyperloop One uses magnetic levitation to lift the train or pod above the tracks. Electric propulsion accelerates it through a low pressure tube. The vehicle is capable of gliding at airline speeds. The promise of this technology is to go 700 to 800 mph.

Elon Musk

Elon Musk originally introduced the concept of the hyperloop. Virgin Hyperloop One says it has made substantial changes to his original concept and plan. The company is very optimistic about rolling the technology out. And there are a lot of benefits: it's an autonomous, enclosed system with no carbon emissions and it cuts travel time, for instance, from LA to San Francisco down to 43 minutes. More work needs to be done to bring these systems into widespread operation, including longer lasting batteries for longer distance trips.

6. Larry Page's Flying Car & Boat

Photo: Courtesy of Kitty Hawk Corporation

The Flier

Flying cars are part of our transportation future. A number of companies are working on prototype models globally. But Google co-founder Larry Page and his company, Kitty Hawk Corporation, have just taken off with their Flyer, a sleek, good looking, one seat, flying car. It's a pleasure craft that doesn't require a pilot license.

Wow Technology

The Flyer is engineered quite differently than other flying car prototypes like Terrafugia's Transition, which is a small plane-car hybrid that runs on gas. The Flyer is powered by ten electric fans along the sides of the craft. On the underside are slim pontoon-like "wheels" for landing. It's designed to fly over water and can stay aloft for 20 minutes. Flyer cruises up to 20 mph and hovers over the water at 3 to 10 feet. It's categorized by the FAA as an ultra-lite craft and consequently doesn't require a pilot's license. It's restricted right now to uncontrolled, remote airspace away from people and is the next generation of Larry Page's flying car program.

A Prototype to Experience the Beauty of Flight

Kitty Hawk designed this prototype as a flying machine for the "pilot" to enjoy the beauty of flight. This is not the prototype generation for urban, mass transit, which the company is committed to delivering. In the Flyer, the "pilot" controls direction and speed. But an onboard computer does the tough stuff like keeping the vehicle level and stable.

7. "Classiest" Flying Car

Image: Courtesy of AeroMobil

AeroMobil 4.0

Fossbytes Review calls this vehicle the world's classiest flying car. AeroMobil, a Slovakia based company, has had it under development for a number of years. They call it a "roadable aircraft" and a flying car. With the AeroMobil 4.0, it's a high flying combo. It's being showcased at global Auto Shows and is set for production in 2020.

Electric VTOL With Umph

AeroMobil 4.0 is in the testing phase right now. What's intriguing is that it delivers "efficient" intra-city travel up to 621 miles, which is more than double what most electric VTOL(Vertical Take-Off and Landing) passenger drone concepts deliver. The company says it has an innovative combustion engine with highly advanced aerospace and automotive technology to achieve efficiency, speed and range over other electric VTOL's.

Highly Advanced Electric, Solar & Combustion Technologies

The vehicle uses a hybrid electric motor on the road supplemented by solar panels on the wings. It has a driving range of 62 miles. Top driving speed is 99 mph and it accelerates from 0 to 62 mph in 10 seconds. In the air, it's powered by a 300 HP combustion engine. The flying range is up to 466 miles and it flies up to 223 mph. There's also an autonomous autopilot system for flight and parachutes in the event of an air emergency.

8. Boeing's Hypersonic Passenger Jet

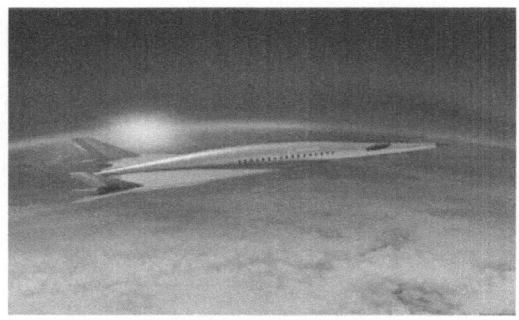

Image: Courtesy of Boeing

Unveiling of World's 1st Hypersonic Passenger Jet Design

Boeing's prototype rendering is the world's first look at commercial hypersonic design and what the jet will look like. The design enables the speed and the speed is awesome.

Travel Times

Boeing's hyper-speed passenger jet can fly from New York to London in 2 hours versus the current 7 hours. Or, how about LA to Japan in 3 hours, versus 11 hours. The design plan is for the jet to fly at Mach 5 or 3800 miles per hour, much faster than its predecessor The Concorde at 1,354 mph.

No Speed Competition

With speeds of Mach 5, Boeing's hypersonic jet has no current competition. The closest competitor is Aerion Corporation. It's high speed passenger plane is expected to reach 1.5 Mach. But, there are many global players working on their design concepts and looking to win the hypersonic flight race.

Hypersonic To-Do List

Much work needs to be done before the high-speed passenger jet takes off. Boeing needs to develop lightweight material for the fuselage to withstand Mach 5 speeds and engines to carry it to Mach 5. The jets will cost billions to develop and build over at least the next 10 years.

Hypersonic Future
Boeing has partnered with the US Department of Defense's Advanced Research Projects Agency DARPA on hypersonic flight for a number of years. Boeing just signed a contract to build for DARPA and the US military the X-37B Spaceplane, the Phantom Express, which takes off vertically and flies at hypersonic speeds, launching satellites into space and then flying back.

9. Flying Motorcycles

Photo: Courtesy of BMW

BMW's Hover Bike

It started as a toy. A Lego, 603 piece kit to build a miniature motorcycle - the BMW R 1200 GS Adventure Bike. The kit was developed by teams from Lego and BMW. BMW engineers were so intrigued by the results, they built the real deal - a flying motorcycle prototype that was first showcased in 2017.

Fast-Forward

BMW engineers have been tweaking the prototype for months. It's now morphing into a new model concept. What we know about the concept vehicle is this. It incorporates BMW Motorrad design with typical components such as a boxer engine and GS silhouette. But engineers have modified the front rim to form a propeller. It appears BMW is working toward commercialization of the flying bike. There's no word on price or timing.

Crowded Skies

There's competition for air space. Besides flying cars and drones, there are a number of prototype flying motorcycles. The Russians have developed one. It's the Russian Hovercraft Scorpion-3 that flies with 4 propellers. They describe it as a single seat aircraft or human carrying drone with a motorcycle seat. Also, a California company Aerofex is testing the Aero X Hoverbike. It's an extraordinary looking hovering bike that, according to trade reports, takes off at $85,000. It flies 10 feet above the ground and travels up to 45 mph. And, it's not just for fun rides. The company claims it has multiple uses including pipeline inspections, cattle herding and search and rescue. It appears flying motorcycle, like flying cars, are accelerating toward our future.

10. Jaguar's Electric Boat

Photo: Courtesy of Jaguar

Electric Boat that Almost Flies

Jaguar just broke another speed record. Not for racing cars. This one is for their electric boat. It just happened recently, shattering the world electric speed record for boat racing. The electric boat is the Jaguar Vector. The racing happened on Coniston Water, the third largest lake in the English Lake District. The Jaguar V makes eco-friendly, green, clean electric water crafts look good for waterways and the environment.

Jaguar Vector Racing

The Jaguar Vector has a V20E electric engine. Electricity provides all the boat's electric power and powers the motor and control systems. The Jaguar V smashed a previous world record of 76.8 mph set a few years ago. The Jaguar V reached and sustained 88.6 mph for 8 miles. The boat was designed and built by Jaguar Vector and their racing partner Williams Advanced Engineering.

Next Race Lap

Jaguar has a strong vision concerning the importance of electric cars and electric boats in the transportation mix of the future. Jaguar says it wants to bring the power and versatility of electrification to the marine industry. Their Jaguar Vector is leading edge in that regard.

11. Where's Your Jet Pack?

Photo: Courtesy of Go Fast Sports

Up, Up and Away

With the intense global R&D underway to bring the first flying car to market, I wondered what the status of jet packs is. They were all the rage earlier in this decade. Turns out, they're still around but haven't matured technologically for widespread commercialization...yet. They are one of the most difficult and complex pieces of flying equipment to engineer. They also remain dangerous to fly.

New Takeoffs with Jet Pack Man

Nick Macomber is known as the Jet Pack Man. He and his jet pack opened the London Olympics, flew over bridges in Ireland and have flown as part of innovation conferences in China. His company Go Fast Sports & Jet Pack International predicts an upcoming renaissance in jet packing. They've created a prototype with a turbine based platform that's capable of flying 30 minutes. That could open up the possibility of commuting to work or school by jetpack.

Weight to Thrust Ratio Challenge

With jet packs, the challenge is weight. Macomber's jet packs weight 65 pounds. When loaded with fuel, hydrogen peroxide, they double in weight. It can catapult you as high as 250 feet, but flight time is around 33 seconds because of the enormous amount of fuel it takes to lift off the ground. The more fuel you add to lengthen the flight, you start reaching the point where you can't get off the ground.

Next Flights

The industry is working on the next generation of jet packs to enable humanity to have their own personal flying machines. Macomber believes the technology will be there in the next couple of years. If so, you'll be able to say good-bye to your daily traffic jammed commute and soar above it.

12. Electric Passenger Planes

Artist Rendering: Zunum Aero

Electric Planes To Revolutionize the Airline Industry With Norway Leading The Way

By 2040, Norway is committed to having all of its short-haul flights, from its airports, on electric aircraft. This is one of the most dramatic government examples of cutting down on carbon dioxide, greenhouse gas emissions from the airline industry.

Booming Industry - 100+ Global Projects

Currently small planes comprise the electric aircraft market. There are no airliner sized electric planes being built. But Norwegian government and aviation industry officials believe that will soon change. Boeing, NASA and Airbus are diligently working on prototype designs. Boeing's Zunum Aero has plans for a 12-seater by 2022 and a 50-seater by 2027. There are more than 100 electric powered aircraft projects currently around the world.

Norway's Plans

Norway's terrain is mountainous and there are many offshore islands. There are many airports because in many cases it's easier to fly to locations. Most flights take 15 to 30 minutes. Norway wants 25 to 30 seat electric planes. And it's determined to have the first electric passenger plane go into service by 2025.

13. China's Hypersonic Jet

Starry Sky
Photo: Courtesy of Chinese Government

Hypersonic Jet That Flies at Mach 6

China has successfully tested its hypersonic aircraft, the XingKong-2, Starry Sky. It reportedly can travel 6-times the speed of sound at Mach 6. Within a few days of the Chinese test, the US Air Force ordered more hypersonic weapons from Lockheed Martin - the 2nd order this year. The global hypersonic tech race is intensely heating up.

Hypersonic Competitors

Russia, China and the US are trying to dominate in hypersonic aircraft and weapons that travel 5 and 6 times the speed of sound. Some military experts believe the Starry Sky can evade existing missile defense systems and potentially carry both conventional and nuclear payloads. They don't expect it to be weaponized for 3 to 5 years. USAF Secretary Heather Walker wants to get hypersonic capability to our military as soon as possible.

Starry Sky Hypersonic Tech

Starry Sky is an experimental hypersonic wave rider that accelerates to Mach 6. It rides the shock waves generated during its supersonic flight. The big concern is that its speed and unpredictable flight trajectories make it very difficult for existing missile defense systems to intercept it. Clearly, this is the beginning of a very big hypersonic aircraft and tech race.

14. Solar Drone Aircraft Powered by Laser Beam

Image of Silent Falcon Courtesy of DARPA

Laser Beams of Power

California-based Silent Falcon UAS Technologies is partnering with the Pentagon's Advanced Research Projects Agency - DARPA - to implement laser power beaming for its solar-electric powered drones. Right now, Silent Falcon drones can fly non-stop 6 hours using batteries and solar energy. They are the only solar electric, long range, long endurance UAS (unmanned aircraft system).

DARPA wants to make the flight time much longer by topping off the batteries via laser beams from the ground. DARPA officials say they're right on the brink of delivering this disruptive technology.

Endless Uses for Endless Flights

What DARPA wants are drones capable of indefinite flight. The drones would engage in sequences of flying and flying while charging from a high powered laser beam directed from the ground. There would be no need to land and refuel. This emerging technology can enable exciting, potential uses such as internet & cellular access in remote areas and for military, search & rescue, wildfire & disaster operations. We're on the brink of power beaming laser technology. This will enable drones in our skies to operate indefinitely. The potential uses are endless.

15. Electric Motorcycles to Debut in 2019

LiveWire

Harley-Davidson is unleashing a slew of new products, with advanced technology, over the next 3 years to pull in a new generation of riders and $1 billion in additional revenues by 2022. The most notable new entry is their electric motorcycle LiveWire.

LiveWires for Young, Urban Commuters Who Prefer Electric

LiveWire opens a completely new market for HD. Young, urban commuters who care about the environment and like electric vehicles that save them money. LiveWire is a no-clutch, "twist and go" electric powered bike. It's coming to market in 2019 and HD is about to provide a first look at the latest prototype in upcoming days.

Biking and Transportation Go Electric

Electric vehicles are reshaping the transportation industry globally from cars to planes. Electric motorcycles are cheaper to operate than gas-powered ones. They're quieter and some don't have gears. There are smaller electric motorcycle brands now on the market, including Zero Motorcycles. The Zero S can go from 0 to 103 mph without shifting gears. They sell an estimated 2000 to 10,000 e-bikes globally a year.

Electric Motorcycle Races

HD recently bought Silicon Valley startup Alta Motors to facilitate development of its electric bikes. HD says they'll rollout additional electric bikes thru 2022. Their intent is to broaden their electric portfolio with lighter, smaller and more accessible product options to convince new riders to give HD a try. Polaris' Indian Motorcycle says it will have an electric motorcycle also available next year. E-biking is getting highly competitive.

16. DARPA's Truck Wheels Change in Motion

Photo: Courtesy of DARPA

DARPA's New Set of Wheels

To see it is to believe it. It's called the Transforming Wheel-Track This is the US Defense Department's Advanced Research Projects Agency DARPA's latest, "go-anyplace, anytime" truck for the US military. It was designed and developed by a team from Carnegie Mellon's National Robotics Engineering Center. It's breakthrough technology that can alter a wheel's shape and function while it's in motion.

Dual Action in 2 Seconds

For soft surfaces, the truck can navigate the terrain on triangular tracks. For hard surfaces, it changes into round wheels for fast travel. The switch can be made in 2 seconds while in motion, which provides soldiers the ability to adjust as needed. Designed for military use, it's also practical for search and rescue missions and construction.

DARPA's X Vehicles

The Transforming Wheel-Track is part of DARPA's Ground X Vehicles technologies program. Besides the shape-shifting wheels, X's highly advanced technologies include in-hub electric motors to increase speed and maneuverability and extreme travel suspension for high speed travel over rough terrain. Also being developed, virtual windows (with 3D goggles) and sensor enhanced virtual perspectives and visual overlays for safe, off-road navigation.

17. Google's Self-Driving Car

Photo: Courtesy of Waymo

Google Project that Self Drives

Waymo is the Google self-driving car project that's now a division of Google's parent Alphabet. It's seems to be leaving other autonomous car makers far behind. You might say, it's in the driver's seat - along with its combo of laser-radars, sensors and software. A ride-hailing program is expected to be launched later this year.

Road Warrior

The Waymo vehicles have done 8 million miles in autonomous driving, including 25,000 miles a day on city streets. The vehicles have 360 degree sensors, radar and software that's designed to detect people, cyclists, vehicles, road work and obstructions up to 3 football fields away. The cars are taught on 8 million miles of real-world traffic and they're about to be commercialized.

Waymo Updates

Waymo has cut a pilot project with Walmart. In the Phoenix area, you can place a Walmart order at a discount and pick it up and take it home in your Waymo driverless car. They have test programs underway with their vehicles in California, Arizona, Texas, Nevada, Michigan and Washington. They also have partnerships with AvisBudget and Autonation.

First All-Electric Jaguars

Waymo is driving the first all-electric Jaguar I-PACE SUVs in the US. They're part of Waymo's test fleet. Waymo expects to add 20,000 I-PACE SUV's to its fleet. They'll be outfitted with the self-driving tech and launched in a ride-hailing service in 2020, joining other vehicles like the Chrysler Pacifica minivan.

18. DARPA's Hypersonic Aircraft

Image of Falcon HTV-2 Courtesy of DARPA

DARPA's Hypersonic Falcon

This is one of DARPA's most amazing, daring and high risk projects. It's called the Falcon Hypersonic Technology Vehicle or Falcon HTV-2. It was designed to overcome the many challenges of hypersonic flight, which is something DARPA is committed to developing. It's a concept vehicle that has helped to pave the way to a hypersonic future.

DARPA's Goal

The end goal is a vehicle that can reach any place in the world in less than an hour. Falcon, designed by Elon Musk's Space X in partnership with DARPA, was designed to go up to Mach 20 or 13,000 miles per hour. That would take you from NYC to LA in 12 minutes.

Lost in Space

Falcon is an unmanned, rocket-launched maneuverable aircraft. Also it's a data-truck with tons of sensors onboard. In a test flight several years ago, showing the difficulty and risks of developing this kind of advanced technology, DARPA harvested only 9 minutes worth of data, before losing contact with the vehicle. The vehicle's development by DARPA remains on hold. But the concepts and goals for hypersonic flight are moving forward with speed, particularly with DARPA's Spaceplane, a new class of vehicles for hypersonic flight.

19. Virgin Galactic Readies for Takeoffs

Image Courtesy of Virgin Galactic

Tech in Sub-orbit with Tourists Onboard

This year, Virgin Galactic's spaceplane climbed 32 miles over California's Mojave Desert in its latest test flight. That crushed all of its previous records. This is the 3rd rocket powered test flight of VSS Unity spaceplane. It brings Sir Richard Branson's Virgin Galactic space tourism company very close to taking its first tourism customers into space.

Amazing Flight

The spaceplane was released from under the wing of its carrier plane at 46,500 feet. VSS Unity fired its rocket motors for 42 seconds to propel itself and the 2 pilots at Mach 2.47 or 2&1/2 times the speed of sound. The spaceplane reached an altitude of 170,800 feet or essentially halfway to outer-space before safely descending to its spaceport in the Mojave Desert. Mission accomplished.

Get Ready for Tourist Takeoffs

Branson is indicating that Virgin Galactic could start commercial flights for space tourists soon, even next year. 800 people have booked at $250,000 each. There's significant competition in this emerging market, including Elon Musk's SpaceX and Jeff Bezos' Blue Origin that offer tourists brief suborbital trips. Bon Voyage!!

20. Smart Cars on Smart Roads

China Photo: "The Solar Expressway"

China's Super-Smart Roads

The Chinese are leading the way to the future of your transportation. It's autonomous vehicles on "intelligent" highways. The smart roads are paved with electric battery rechargers, mapping sensors and solar panels. The rechargers will repower electric cars as they drive along. Some call China's super intelligent highway "the Solar Expressway".

Tests Now Underway on the Solar Expressway

China's smart road has been built in the city of Jinan. It's 3,540 feet long and the technologies are being embedded under transparent concrete. The solar panels that are already embedded generate enough electricity to power highway lights and 800 nearby homes. 45,000 vehicles barrel down the smart highway daily.

Made in China 2025 Masterplan

This Chinese smart highway is the road to our transportation future. It's part of President Xi Jinping's plan to make China an advanced manufacturing, technology and innovation power by 2025. It's a smart, solar powered road to the future of smart cars. It costs about $6.5 million.

21. NextGen Flying By Hexacopter

TEAM
BLUE SPARROW

DEVICE
BLUE SPARROW

Artist Rendering: Penn State

Penn State's Hexacopter

It definitely looks like a highly advanced helicopter. It's a hexacopter created by a team of Penn State engineers led by Associate Professor of Aerospace Engineering Jack Langelaan. It's their winning design concept and technical specifications that landed them in a top ten contender spot in Boeing's GoFly International Competition for safe, small personal flying machines with vertical takeoff and landing and minimal noise. The competition underscores Boeing's belief that personal flight vehicles are part of the transportation future.

Rotor Power

6 rotors give the Blue Sparrow thrust. The team gets flight control by modulating the rotor speeds. That changes the thrust from each rotor and the torque from each rotor. The total thrust controls acceleration. Differential thrust and torque give them control over pitch, roll and yaw.

The rubber is now hitting the road for the Blue Sparrow. Team Captain Langelaan says the GoFly criteria to place in the Top Ten was rigorous and difficult. Next steps are to finish building the prototype and start test flying the Blue Sparrow.

22. Ingenious Flying Car

Image: Courtesy of University of Kansas

The Mamba Flying Car

There's elegance to the design of this exceptional flying vehicle. And a focus on safety. It's Team Mamba's Device Mamba. The team started off with the idea of creating a vehicle to be sold as a flying motorcycle. That morphed into what they say looks like the head of a snake, according to University of Kansas team leader Lauren Schumacher. Hence, it's the Mamba with style, design and vertical lift.

Hexacopter

Mamba is a winning flying car. It's a hexacopter with 6 ducted fans to enable it to hover. To move forward, 2 aft ducts provide thrust.

Safety First

Team Mamba has put safety as its' #1 component for design. They think one failure or death could shut down this newly emerging industry of personal flying vehicles. Their design is a top ten contender in Boeing's Go Fly International Competition.

23 Flying Car-Off-Road Vehicle

Image Courtesy of Trek Aerospace

FLYKART 2

This vehicle was inspired by go-carts. It's the creation of Trek Aerospace, a California engineering firm that specializes in fan powered watercraft and aircraft. FlyKart 2 is an off-road vehicle that can also takeoff and fly. The company calls it a fun off-roader that soars.

Very High Tech

The vehicle is all-electric. 10 ducted propellers provide vertical takeoff. The entire aircraft leans forward to cruise inflight. All of the vehicle's movements are controlled through the thrusts from the propellers.

On the Cusp of the Flying Future

Team Trek Aerospace believes the FlyKart 2 is one of many potential flying vehicles in the future. They believe we're just at the start of what electric aircraft with distributed propulsion can do. The FlyKart 2 placed top ten in Boeing's GoFly international competition.

24. Populist Personal Flight

Image: Courtesy of AEROXO LV

ERA Aviabike

It's called ERA Aviabike. Team AEROXO LV of Latvia approached Boeing's GoFly international competition with practicality. They wanted to create a personal flying machine with sizzle and appeal that would sell to global bikers. The global motorbike market is huge. Their concept design and technical specifications have won them a top ten spot in the contest. Like the 9 other competitors, they're now building their concept into a real, flying prototype. After that, the journey to global sales.

Combo Bike, Helicopter & Plane

The team describes it as a "tilt rotor aerial vehicle". It takes off like a helicopter then tilts its motors so it flies like a fixed wing plane. It looks like a science fiction motorcycle that's ready to fly.

Green, Affordable and Autonomous if You Like

ERA Aviabike is all-electric right now. But other power sources going forward are options. Also, you can fly in full autonomous mode or be computer assisted. This team also thinks about cost and pricing. They've designed it to be affordable and not just a toy for billionaires.

Steps to Takeoff

Latvia's prototype vehicle, like the 9 other international contenders, now has to meet a series of thresholds that include safety, low noise, vertical takeoffs and landings, small size and minimum 20 mile non-stop flights.

25. Dutch Personal Flying Machine

Image: Courtesy of SILVERWING

SILVERWING

Dutch team SILVERWING designed this personal flying machine that's an international winner. It's another top ten contender in Boeing's GoFy International Competition. They've created a flying motorcycle made airborne by 2 large rotors. The rotors are driven by 2 electric motors.

Increased Comfort Level

Team SILVERWING designed S1 from the rider's comfort level perspective and to clear the rigorous competitive standards set by Boeing GoFly. The standards include safety, vehicle size, vertical takeoff and landing, noise level, payload and line of sight. SILVERWING says the biggest challenge was to keep the noise level minimal while being able to carry a person.

S1 Specs

S1 takes off vertically. The thrust for liftoff is provided by the 2 rotors, powered by electric motors. It then transitions to horizontal flight like a plane.

You Can Fly It

The Dutch team says even if you aren't familiar with the dynamics of flight, you'll understand and be able to fly their S1. They believe they've designed something people are willing to ride/fly and make the dream of personal flight a reality. Like the other Boeing GoFly Top Ten competitors, they're now building their working prototype to fly.

26. MIT's Drone Boat

Photo: Courtesy of MIT

Driverless Boats

An MIT team has developed a fleet of driverless boats. They can ferry goods, people and monitor traffic and the environment.. This could help free-up road congestion in waterway enriched areas like Venice, Amsterdam, Miami and Bangkok. The autonomous boats operate with precise control and high maneuverability.

Autonomous Waterways

Scientists envision a future where driverless boats can perform city services overnight, further reducing congestion. For instance, deliveries and waste management could be performed at night, which would reduce daytime traffic. But, there's a lot more than that.

3D Printed Boats that Can Self-Assemble Into Bridges & Concert Stages

The boats are roughly 4 by 2 meters. They are extremely high-tech. They contain location trackers, sensors, microcontrollers and other hardware. They can be programmed to self-assemble into platforms for food markets, floating bridges, connect stages and forums in just a few hours.

Amazing Tech

MIT researchers 3D printed the rectangular hull with a commercial printer. That produced 16 separate sections that were spliced together. The hull was sealed by several layers of fiberglass. The hull contains a power supply, GPS, WIFI, antenna, minicomputer and microcontroller. The team says they're inexpensive to manufacture. These driverless boats can be used for transportation, possibly cutting congestion on our highways. And besides ferrying people and goods back and forth on water, they can be equipped with environmental sensors to monitor water, air and human health conditions.

27. Easy to Fly Personal Flying Machine

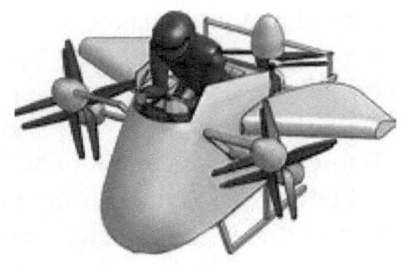

Image: Courtesy of USA Team Snoop

Y6 Tilt Rotor

It's a Y6 tilt rotor with wing, hybrid powertrain and a cruising speed of 70 knots. The Pegasus 1 is a top 10 winner in Boeing's GoFly International. It's the creation of USA Team Scoop and Captain Alex Smolen, who is a self-taught programmer with experience flying and building multicopters.

Personal Flight

Smolen sees the Pegasus as the first step toward fun and simple personal flight. He thinks anyone can fly the vehicle for 30 minutes and will find it a wonder to fly.

Tech Specs

The vehicle has 6 propellers. When it hovers, they lift Pegasus off the ground, slowly and in any direction like a drone. To cruise, the propellers tilt giving it lift and thrust. As it accelerates, the wings give additional lift making it fly like a plane.

Pegasus 1 Promise

Team Scoop and Alex Smolen are now building their concept into a flyable prototype. They say Pegasus 1 is safe, easy to use and a wonder to fly.

28. Japan's Personal Flying Machine

Image: Courtesy of Team Tetra

Tetra 3

This Boeing GoFly, Top Ten winner is so cool it looks like its ready for Star Wars adventures. It's called Tetra 3 and is the concept design created by Team Tetra of Japan. It clearly looks like a flying motorbike. The operator rides it like a motorcycle. And according to Team Tetra Captain Tasuka Nakai, the operator can work it and fly it like a video game.

Fun and Easy to Fly

The Japanese team says the Tetra 3 is easy for anyone to fly. An electric motor powers the propellers. The device can hover, take off and land vertically and fly horizontally, much like a plane with fixed wings.

Takeoff Time

The rubber is hitting the road. The futuristic, Star Wars-like Tetra 3 is now being built into a working prototype to fly for the gold.

29. British Personal Flying Machine

Image: Courtesy of Team Leap

The Vantage

The captain of the British team Leap defines their personal flying machine The Vantage as a 5-rotor air bike. It's also a top ten contender in Boeing's GoFly International Competition of personal flying machine prototypes.

Loaded with Engineering

This concept's design and technical specifications are stunning. It has an internal combustion engine that produces electric power from a generator. 5 electric motors drive a rotor that keeps Vantage airborne. 2 more rotor-motor combos give it forward thrust. And each rotor can be controlled independently.

Real Deal - No Fairy Dust

Captain Bruno Howard says "no need for fairy dust". It's made of real components you can buy today. He adds the principles of safety, controllability and redundancy are built into its design. Team Leap is now building a working prototype with vertical takeoff and landing, low noise, able to fly non-stop 20 miles, safe and small (under 8.5 feet).

30. Georgia Tech's Flying Car

Image Courtesy of Georgia Tech

Georgia Tech's Flying Car

It's a personal flying vehicle with distinctive design and technical specifications that won top 10 status in Boeing's GoFly International Personal Flying Machine competition. The Hummingbuzz is straight out of Georgia Tech.

All Electric Flying Fan

True, it looks like a flying fan with a motorcycle on top of it. The rider sits on top of the motor bike that also houses a battery pack. The vehicle is an all-electric, ducted fan equipped with counter-rotating coaxial rotors.

Boeing

Boeing believes that personal flying machines will be part of the transportation mix in the not-to-distant future. That's one of the reasons for their annual GoFly international competition. The Georgia Tech team is developing a working prototype vehicle from their design and technical specifications. The vehicle must have vertical take-off and landing, be safe, travel non-stop at least 20 miles, not be loud and be less than 8.5 feet in length.

31. NASA's Unmanned Aircraft

Photo: Courtesy of NASA

Ikhana – Flying Drone Aircraft

NASA has recently flown a large aircraft that is remotely-piloted unaccompanied in commercial airspace. It's called Ikhana and it flew through Class-A airspace where commercial airlines fly. Large, unmanned aircraft that are remotely piloted like Ikhana have required a safety chase aircraft as it travels through airspace used by commercial planes. Not so for Ikhana.

Great Significance

NASA worked closely with the FAA for months to ensure safety and a successful maiden flight. It went off without a hitch and moves the US steps closer to normalizing unmanned aircraft operations in the commercial and private pilot airspace.

New Roles for Unmanned Aircraft like Ikhana

This successful flight opens the doors to service roles like fighting forest fires and new emergency search and rescue operations. According to NASA test pilot Scott Howe, "We're flying with a suite of sophisticated technology that greatly enhances the safety capabilities of pilots flying big unmanned aircraft in the National Airspace System".

Historic Flight

NASA has called this historic flight a milestone for their Unmanned Aircraft Systems Integration in the National Aerospace Systems. The flight took off from Edwards Air Force base in California. It entered Class A airspace of commercial airlines at about 20,000 feet and Class E at about 10,000 feet where general aviation pilots fly.

32. Not Your Average Flying Machine

Image: Courtesy of Texas A&M

The Harmony

Forget the jetpack. The future of personal flying machines looks quite different, as in Texas A&M's The Harmony pictured above. This flying machine is one of ten winners in Boeing's GoFly international competition. The Texans will be turning the concept into a working prototype.

The Harmony's Green and All-Electric

The all-electric vehicle was created by Texas A&M engineers. It's distinctive to say the least. It's egg-shaped and looks a bit like a lectern. The engineers call it a personal rotorcraft. The pilot sits above the open coaxial rotors. The creators say the configuration maximizes hover and forward flight flexibility, pilot safety and reliability. The Texans says it's practical, safe, green and efficient. The next step is to take their winning technical specifications and design and build a prototype to fly.

33. Where's the US in the Bullet Train Race?

World's Fastest Bullet Train - Japan's Loseries SC Maglev

Asia Dominates

Asia and Europe are dominating in speed and deployment of bullet trains. The world leaders in the technology are Japan, France and China. These nations have systems up and running and some are currently building more. Here's the 2018 list of the Top Five Fastest Bullet Trains in the World:

1. Japan - Loseries SC Maglev, also known as Japan Laser, at 375 mph
2. France - TGV at 357 mph
3. China - CRH38OA at 302 mph
4. Japan - N700 Shinkansen 275 mph
5. China - Shanghai Maglev at 275 mph

Massive Acceleration Testing

Some of these systems have exceeded speeds of 400 mph with belief they'll be able to sustain travel at 500 mph. That would cut a trip from Paris to Berlin to 2 hours, very comparable to air travel.

Where's Bullet Team USA?

Two big questions: where is the US and why isn't it a leader in this important, real-time intercity travel technology. True, we have Elon Musk developing his HyperLoop which, when implemented, should outclass and out-race bullet trains. It's expected to travel in its vacuum tube at 700 mph. But why hasn't the US invested in bullet trains like China, Japan and France have. Likely reasons, money and government funding budgets. These systems are super-expensive tech & infrastructure projects. Government and corporate leaders have to believe in its future profitability.

34. NASA's Supersonic Passenger Jet

Courtesy NASA: NASA'S X-59 QueSST

X-Plane Takeoff: SST with No Boom

NASA and Lockheed Martin just reached an important milestone on their quieter supersonic X-plane. They've completed the initial design on a low boom SST passenger jet. Why is that significant to all of us? How would you like to hop on a plane and go from NYC to LA in 2 hours? Or, NYC to London in 3 hours. That's what the X-plane is all about. Some aviators are calling it "Son of Concorde", after the famed Anglo-French SST that was decommissioned 15 years ago. But, this one has NASA expertise.

Supersonic Getaways on QueSST

NASA calls it the X-59 QueSST. The Quiet Supersonic Transport that travels at 1100 mph. They just crossed a key threshold to make supersonic flight over land a real possibility. They've completed a preliminary design review for the low boom flight experimental plane, the X-Plane.

Looking and Sounding Good

NASA thinks it has what it needs. They say QueSST can fly at supersonic speeds and create a soft thump rather than a loud sonic boom that's associated with SST flights. QueSST is going to be flown over communities to collect data for regulators to okay SST flights over land in the US and globally. In fact, in November, an F-18 fighter jet is going to go supersonic and fire off the "sonic thump" over Galveston, Texas to gauge noise reaction from the public.

Testing Phase Underway

Actual flight tests are expected in 2021. But, over the next few months, low-speed wind tunnel testing and what's called static inlet performance tests will be taking place at NASA's Langley Research Center in Virginia. In May, a scale model of the X-plane successfully passed a supersonic wind tunnel at NASA's Glenn Research Center in Ohio. NASA is moving with supersonic speed on this program.

35. Hyperloop Gets Real

Image: Courtesy of Hyperloop One

Get Ready for the Ride of Your Life

Thanks to the combination of Elon Musk's concept and Sir Richard Branson's investment, the hyperloop is nearing reality. The hyperloop is a pod placed inside a vacuum-sealed tube. By levitating the pod, friction is dramatically reduced which allows exponentially increased speed. This technology combination allows for possible speeds of 700-800 miles per hour.

Global Hyperloop Competition

Entrepreneurs globally are attempting to duplicate Elon Musk's vision of hyperloop travel. A Spanish company Zeleros says their hyperloop system is capable of 745 mph. This will allow travel from Madrid to Paris in about an hour, rather than 12 hours drive time. There are at least ten hyperloop concept routes around the world conducting feasibility studies. They include some in the UK, US, India, Canada and Mexico.

Hyperloop Standout in the Fast Lane

The one hyperloop route that is ahead of the pact is the one between Pittsburgh, Columbus and Chicago by Virgin Hyperloop One, which is a Richard Branson company. It's the first route to hire consultants for environmental as well as feasibility studies. This puts it years ahead of other hyperloop projects. Travel from Pittsburgh to Chicago on the hyperloop is estimated to be 45 minutes rather than a 7 hour drive time. The studies for Virgin Hyperloop One will look at the impact on wildlife as well as the infrastructure needed such as tunneling, tubes and pylons. The hope is to use rail and highway right of ways to facilitate deployment.

36. Dutch Flying Car

Image Courtesy of PAL-V

Henry Ford

In 1927, Henry Ford said: "Mark my words. A combination airplane and motor car is coming. You may smile, but it will come." Talk about a futurist! He was right on, off by about 90 years, but the time is now.

The Liberty: Ready for Production, Take-off and Driving

This is a hot prototype flying car we wanted to focus on. It's the creation of the Netherlands based company PAL-V. Called The Liberty, the developers claim it's production ready, making it a global first. And they say it's "Licensed to Thrill".

Distinctive Design

As you can see in the artist's rendering, the Liberty has a design that's different from other flying car prototypes. It looks like a helicopter. And, in fact, there's a center mounted rotor blade on top. The big deal is that it is production ready. All it awaits is full certification, which it expects in 2019. The company says it will start delivering vehicles shortly thereafter.

Speed Ups

On the road, it can drive up to 100 mph and accelerate from 0 to 62 mph in under 9 seconds. The car component has a 100 HP engine. The aircraft component has a 200 HP engine with top speed of 120 mph and a range of 310 miles or 4.3 hours. Maximum altitude is 11,500 feet. It's a 2-seater The Dutch have priced it at $599,000 for the top of the line model and $399,000 for a sports vehicle model.

In the Skies and On the Highways

The Liberty and the AeroMobile 4.0 are cited by a number of industry watchers as the first two flying cars to enter the airspace and hiways commercially. No question, Henry Ford would be one of the first driver-pilots of a flying car.

37. Your Flying Taxi is Here

Photo of Pop.up Next: Courtesy of Airbus

Pop.up Next: Audi - Airbus Collaboration

It's rush hour. Traffic is at a standstill. Then, out of the sky, it's your flying taxi. That's the promise of Pop.up Next. There are numerous flying taxi projects underway such as the Chinese EHay, Volocopter and Uber's Elevate machine. However, Pop.up Next has the backing of and is a collaboration among engineering greats Audi, Airbus and also the German government.

Electric & Autonomous Flying-Driving Machine

Pop.up Next is part car and part quadcopter. It is electric powered and has autonomous technology. There are still many engineering challenges for Pop.up Next. But, the German government has approved testing the flying taxi in and around the German city of Ingolstadt, which is Audi's headquarters. In a statement by the German Transport Ministry: "Flying taxis aren't a vision any longer. They can take us off into a new dimension of mobility."

Pop.up and Let It Go

As you can see in the prototype picture, Pop.up Next is comprised of two main parts. The ground component, which is a futuristic looking, 2-seat car. And the drone module, which connects to the top of the car to fly it off to its destination. Both modules operate with autonomous technology. The passengers program where they want to go and the machines do the rest. Passengers can sit back and relax.

New Vision of Urban Travel

The creators of Pop.up Next believe flying taxis will give time back to commuters, free them of the need to drive, "through a flexible, shared and adaptable new way of moving within cities." So, in the future, when you hail a taxi, it may be a taxi in the skies.

38. USAF Secret Space Ship

Photo: Courtesy of USAF

Secret Space Plane

The US Air Force has a top secret space plane X-37B recently spotted by sky watchers over Edinburgh, Scotland and The Netherlands. This would be the OTV's (Orbital Test Vehicle) 5th top secret mission. The big questions are: what's the mission and what's in the payload? What we do know is that the space plane was manufactured by Boeing and its technology is outstanding.

Supersonic Robotic Orbiter

The plane's speed is supersonic. It flies 110 to 500 miles above the earth. X-37B is unmanned and robotic. We know it was launched late last year from NASA's Kennedy Space Center at Cape Canaveral. One of Elon Musk's SpaceX Falcon 9 rockets carried it into launch and orbit. It has had more than 2000 days in orbit during its 5 missions. Each mission is designed to break the previous endurance record.

Secret Missions - Secret Payloads

No one other than the USAF, NASA and possibly Elon Musk's SpaceX knows what X-37B's classified missions fully entail. Some observers have speculated it's carrying a space weapon. We do know its missions deliver technology demonstrations. On this mission, the USAF disclosed it's carrying small satellite ride shares. It's also designed to demonstrate greater opportunities for rapid space access. And there will be on-orbit testing of emerging space technologies. The USAF's ASETS-11 (Advanced Structurally

Embedded Thermal Spreader) is onboard. It tests experimental electronics and oscillating thermal pipes. No word on the results. That's still in orbit.

39. DARPA's Robot Ship

Photo: Courtesy of DARPA

The SEA Hunter

The US Defense Department's Advanced Research Projects Agency - DARPA - has developed a "ghost" ship. It's called SEA Hunter and has an all-robotic crew. No humans allowed on board. It's the first prototype of an autonomous, robotic sub hunting ship. It's been christened and is now being tested, deployed and developed by the Office of Naval Research. It gives new meaning to Wagner's Opera "The Flying Dutchman".

SEA Hunter's Awesome Technology

Robo ship uses a 5th generation medium frequency sonar system mounted on the hull. It conducts both active and passive sonar passes. DARPA is also working on the development of nonconventional sensor technology to further enable the vessel to precisely spot and track enemy subs, mines and vessels on the high seas.

Revolutionary Prototype

DARPA believes SEA Hunter is a revolutionary prototype vehicle that could ultimately lead to a new class of ocean going vessels with no people on board. The ship and its all-robot crew have undergone extensive open sea trials for long range tracking capabilities. It's also been successfully tested with a mine countermeasure payload.

Oceanic Vision With a Good Price

The goal of this program is for a future in which manned warships and robot vessels complement each other on diverse missions. Robot ship is very cost effective. It costs $15,000 to $20,000 per day to operate $700,000 a day it takes to operate a guided missile destroyer.

40. Electric-Powered Planes

Artist Rendering: Zunum Aero Electric Plane

Climate Change

The signs of climate change are all around us. Extreme weather, rising sea levels, melting polar icecaps, deadly disease outbreaks, severe environmental stress on animals. . A major contributor is global aircraft exhaust. Enter a solution - the dawn of electric powered planes.

Take-Offs

Current aircraft spew 500 million tons of CO_2 into the atmosphere every year. Scientists warn if the amount of CO_2 isn't cut 80% by 2050, it will be disastrous. As it stands right now, the amount of CO_2 is expected to triple by mid-century. By contrast, electric planes spew no CO_2. They are clean, green technology and can be cheap to operate. An example is the 2-seat e-Genius. It successfully flew over the Alps. The operational cost of flying 300 miles is $15.00. But the bigger the e-plane, the more expensive it is to operate. That's why the industry is turning to hybrid e-planes.

Hybrid Approach

Zunum Aero just received an order from JetSuite for 100 hybrid electric planes. Delivery is 2020. The 12 seat aircrafts are like a Prius, partially electric. Zunum is a startup, backed by JetBlue Technology Ventures and Boeing Horizon X. Both Boeing and JetBlue are banking on hybrid e-planes before all electric aircraft become widely used. The hybrid is eco-friendly. It produces 80% to 100% less carbon emissions than traditional aircraft. Zunum and an Israeli company Eviation with a 9 seat all electric aircraft, plan on test flights of the e-planes in 2019. The goal is to make these planes faster, cheaper and much more eco-friendly than current airplane fleets. Experts predict that by 2035 all electric planes will be carrying 100 plus passengers routinely. Between now and then the energy storage problem has to be solved.

41. DARPA's Flying Truck

Artist Rendering: Courtesy of DARPA

ARES

Flying trucks for US combat troops in the midst of battle. The US Defense Department's Advanced Research Projects Agency, DARPA, has an ambitious program well underway to rapidly supply and also evacuate troops in volatile circumstances with flying trucks. The code name is ARES, Aerial Reconfigurable Enabled Systems. It's developing vehicles that drive and fly nimbly and with speed. ARES is part of DARPA's Transformer program which has been very successful in the development of flying cars.

ARES Awesome Military Technology

DARPA's flying trucks are dual-function vehicles for high speed vertical takeoffs and landings. They hover and land with two tilting fans. The vehicles are capable of high speeds during flight. To reduce ground threats, DARPA researchers focus on unmanned, autonomous aerial logistics systems. Aerial threat evasion from, for example surface to air missiles, is being built in. Also resistance to IED (Improvised Explosive Devices) is a priority for the vehicles.

Reducing Risks

The military importance of this program is significant. Ground transportation in combat areas is highly dangerous. The trucks are subject to ambush and IED's. Primary purpose of ARES is to cut risks to logistical deliveries for combat troops. Those deliveries are substantial. US combat outposts require 100,000 pounds of material every week. There are also world highway applications. The flying truck has significant commercial applications globally.

42. DARPA's Space Plane

DARPA's Hypersonic Space Plane

It's called the Phantom Express or XS-1. A space plane that launches satellites at a minute's notice. The US Defense Department's Advanced Research Projects Agency - DARPA - is spearheading the concept. Boeing is building it for test flights in 2020.

Hypersonic

The Phantom Express flies at hypersonic speeds up to Mach 10 or 7,600 miles per hour. It climbs to an altitude of 12,250 kilometers (7,611 miles) and higher. It's an experimental space plane/booster. The vehicle does vertical takeoffs and horizontal landings. DARPA designed it to launch small satellites for the US military.

Robotic and Reusable

XS-1 is unmanned, robotic and reusable. It's neither a traditional aircraft nor a conventional satellite launch system. It's a hybrid of both. DARPA's mission for XS-1 is to cut satellite launch costs by a factor of ten. Also, to greatly cut wait times between launches.

Mission Possible

Phantom Express has some hurdles to clear. Specifically, meeting several key DARPA goals. The Agency wants one day turnarounds including 10 satellite launches in 10 days. It will undergo rigorous tests flights in about three years.

Innovation at Hypersonic Speed

Here's how it works. XS-1 is a two-part vehicle. The reusable space plane vehicle flies at hypersonic speed to suborbital altitudes. Then the plane deploys a disposable secondary rocket. The rocket separates from the vehicle and launches the satellites into orbit. DARPA wants the Phantom Express to do another satellite launch within hours of the first.

43. Orbiting Space Hotels

Image: Courtesy of Orion Span

Out of this World

In 2022, you can take a 12 day vacation in space. Houston, TX based Orion Span is developing the world's first luxury space hotel It's called the Aurora Station. And the first 4 months of orbit aboard Aurora are sold out. $80,000 per passenger deposits came from North America, Europe and the Middle East. Actual 12 day vacation packages start at $9.5 million. Orion plans to launch the space module in 2021 and put the first guests into orbit in 2022.

Close Quarters - Not Much Space

Aurora accommodates 4 passengers and a 2 member crew of astronauts. The station is 43.5 feet long and 14 feet wide. The International Space Station is 8 times that size. It orbits at an altitude of 200 miles above the earth every 90 minutes. So passengers would see 16 sunrises and 16 sunsets per day. Passengers must complete a 3 month astronaut training program at Orion in order to get on board.

Orbital Experience

It would be an experience of a lifetime. 12 days of zero gravity and flying freely around the space station. The space hotel has many windows from which passengers would enjoy the northern and southern auroras. They'll participate in research experiments like growing food in space. And they can live stream their vacation back home via high speed, wireless internet access.

Space Condos - The Sky's the Limit

Orion Span is operated by seasoned space professionals, innovators and entrepreneurs. Besides operating as a luxury hotel, it can be chartered to space agencies. According to operators, it will also serve as a center for zero gravity research and space manufacturing. The station is modular and easily expanded. Operators expect to sell dedicated housing units as the world's first space condos. This is crowded space that includes competitors like Elon Musk and Richard Branson.

44. Flying, Driving Drones

Photo: Courtesy of MIT

Flying, Driving Drones

From the MIT roboticists who created the world's first flying monkey comes flying, driving drones. Roboticists at MIT's Computer Science and Artificial Intelligence Laboratory have developed a quadcopter drone with wheels. It drives and flies autonomously. The drones can swarm in groups. And they can do so without colliding into each other. There's an important innovation breakthrough here. Current drone robots that are good at one form of transportation aren't good at another. The MIT drone is good at both flying and driving.

Flying Monkeys

This same team of roboticists previously created a robot called the "flying monkey". The monkey flies, runs and grasps objects. But it isn't autonomous. The researchers program its paths. It can't safely travel on its own. But it has served as a foundation for the roboticists' next iteration on their innovation theme - flying, driving drones.

Flying Cars

The MIT scientists call their flying, driving drone a "flying car." They've developed eight, 4-motored quadcopter drones. The drones have 2 small motors with wheels at their base. In simulations they drive 825 feet and fly 300 feet before their batteries run out. The researchers believe these hybrid drones are more efficient and versatile drone vehicles than those that only drive or fly. And the hybrid quadcopters allow the researchers to test multiple concepts for flying cars.

45. Charged Roads for Electric Cars

Charged Roads to Power Electric Cars

It's an environmental dream come true. Battery charging highways that wirelessly power electric cars as they drive along. . Bottom-line: electric cars would be a long distance practicality.

Game Changing Innovation Research

Stanford University has the project on the road. Researchers are working on a new wireless power system embedded right beneath the surface of the road. The wirelessly charged roads would power the electric car while it moves along the highway to its destination. This important concept could result in widespread use of electric cars.

New Wireless Charger

Stanford researchers have produced a wireless charger that does something other wireless chargers don't. The charger automatically calibrates the radio wave frequency. That's the medium that transfers the power. The tuning calibration is in sync with charges in the distance between the charging pad and the car, enabling the power transfer.

Power Results

The system has been tested in computer simulations and in experiments using a LED light bulb. The power results were great. The team found the system transfers power with 100% efficiency up to a 27 inch distance between the road and the vehicle. That distance spread is perfect for electric cars. The car's floor is about 8 inches above the road and the chargers are right beneath the surface.

Bright Future with Some Questions

Some experts question if the system will work if the power coil is fixed and the other component, the car, is moving which it would be.

46. Helicopter Cars

Photo: Courtesy of Terrafugia

TFX Flying Car Concept

Your dream commuter car is coming to your driveway. TFX, the prototype flying car that takes off and lands like a helicopter. It's brand new automotive and aviation innovation. You vertically take off from your driveway and land vertically in your office parking lot. It also drives like a car on the road. One of the selling points of the helicopter car is you can avoid and take-off from traffic jams.

TFX is autonomous, electric and fuel efficient. Vertical takeoff and landing means no need for an airport. Chinese owned company Terrafugia says the vehicle will be on the roads and in the skies within ten years. Company founder Dr. Carl Dietrich and his team of MIT engineers created the world's first FAA and NTSB approved flying car The Transition. They designed and engineered the TFX.

Pushing Flying Car Technology Skywards

Meanwhile, NASA and Uber are teaming up to make electric flying cars operational within six years. Their dual vision is flying taxis for cities. NASA has developed air traffic management for a fleet of flying taxis. Uber has shared its plans for a ridesharing network and NASA is going to test it through simulations. NASA believes the process will help develop needed industry standards and regulations.

NASA-Uber

Here's the NASA-Uber concept. Flying taxis that are affordable and deployed in urban areas. Among other compelling points, the electric and autonomous flying taxis would reduce air pollution and traffic congestion. NASA has a traffic management plan for flying cars. It's a powerful combination to launch flying taxes on the roads and in the sky. NASA and Uber are now building plans for ridesharing networks. Rides will be booked through the Uber app, just like Uber cars. The networks will be operational by 2023.

47. Terrafugia's TF-2

Courtesy of Terrafugia: TF-2 Concept

Plane and Ground Vehicle

Terrafugia invented the world's 1st FAA and NTSB approved flying car, The Transition. The TF-2 is a next generation concept design they're working on now. It promises door to door service for 4 passengers and their luggage. There's a detachable pod. It goes from a flight vehicle to a ground vehicle in 2 minutes.

Going to Market

The TF-2 will enter the market as a hybrid electric aircraft that will be flown by a pilot. But as the technology they're working on matures, the plan is to go all electric and with autonomous systems. At the moment the company says the maximum cruising speed is 240 km/hr. The cost per hour of flight is $400. No time frame for launch has been announced.

China, Sweden & US

US based Terrafugia has a deep pockets parent company Geely of China and its "sister" company Volvo of Sweden is also owned by Geely. The three are launching The Transition in 2019. It's the world's first FAA and NTSB approved flying car.

48. Tiny Robot With Applicatios for Drones

New Robot Mimics Insect Flight

Researchers at Delft University of Technology in The Netherlands have developed a novel flying robot that mimics the flight control and dynamics of insects. Its flying wings beat 17 times per second. And it generates enough force to stay airborne and controls the flight by slight changes in wing motion.

DelFly Nimble

The engineers have named it DelFly Nimble. The tiny robot is autonomous. It can hover on the spot, do 360° flips and fly any direction with agility like an insect. Right now it has top speeds of 15.5 mph and excellent power efficiency with a flight range of 1 km on a fully charged battery.

Important Applications

DelFly Nimble has exceptional flight qualities which open up new drone applications. Scientists say it's also exceptionally well suited to advance biological and engineering research into insects and their flight control and dynamics.

49. Elon Musk's Loop Lift

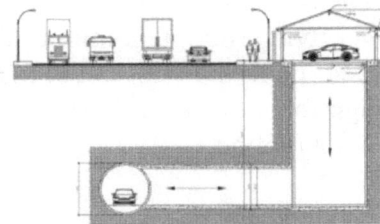

Boring Co.'s Tunnel and Lift

Boring Company's Loop Lift

Hawthorne City, CA City Council just gave Elon Musk and his Boring Company the okay to build a proof of concept prototype of his Loop Lift. The concept involves an elevator lift to connect, for the test, a ground level garage to an underground Hyperloop tunnel.

Specifics

The plan is to connect a one mile long Hyperloop tunnel that's on the campus of Musk's Space X to a private house that's owned by a Musk company. The vision is to cut future traffic from the roads by parking vehicles in underground tunnels and then, for this test, connecting them to the Hyperloop transportation system by elevator lifts.

Musk's Vision of the Loop Lift, Hyperloop and Flying Cars

Musk envisions a network of underground tunnels and elevator lifts built in the basements of homes, office buildings, malls, you name it. He believes that the key to cutting traffic gridlocks in major cities is a large number of underground tunnels for vehicles, connecting to high speed transport like the Hyperloop which has the potential of travelling 700 to 800 mph. He adds flying cars into the mix. All, to start cutting road traffic, the growing need for vehicle parking spaces and gridlock.

50. High Tech Champagne in Space

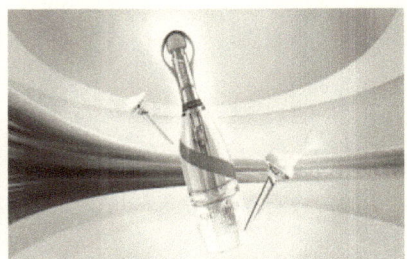

Photo: Courtesy of Mumm

Orbiting Champagne for Space Tourists at Zero Gravity

Future space tourists on the journey of their lifetime may have the added adventure of sipping champagne in orbit. In terms of technology, that's not an easy thing to provide at zero gravity. A French designer/innovator Octave de Gaulle has designed a bottle to dispense champagne at zero gravity.

Airbus Testing It

It's being tested by an Airbus Zero-G plane that makes deep climbs and dives to create 20 second intervals of weightlessness. That puts the bottle to the test to see if it works and dispenses champagne at zero gravity in space.

This Tech Not for Astronauts

US astronauts are not allowed to consume alcohol in space. This is being designed for future adventurous tourists who travel to space. Concerning the tech: the wine, in the upper portion of the bottle is released by a finger controlled valve that uses the champagne's own carbon dioxide to drive out small amounts of foam. So in space, you'd be sipping foam champagne. Cheers!

51. World First & No Emissions

Germany's Hydrogen Train

Emission Free Rail Travel

The train is officially called the Coradia iLint. It's clean energy rolling through northern Germany. It just started regular passenger service in the Lower Saxony Region. This is the first time that commercial trains powered by hydrogen-based cells have gone into use for passengers.

French Manufacturer

Two trains are in service. 14 more are on order for 2021. They're being manufactured by French based Alstom, which is one of Europe's biggest railway manufacturers. The hydrogen trains are being touted as important innovation delivered by Germany and France.

Train Green Tech

The trains are low noise, have zero emissions and can reach speeds of 140 kmh. Germany specifically invested in them to reduce diesel fuel train emissions. The fuel cells convert hydrogen and oxygen into electricity to power the trains.

Many Advantages Over Diesel

The trains are refueled at a mobile hydrogen fill-up station next to the tracks in Bremervoerde, Germany. They are much more efficient than diesel. One tank of the hydrogen train can run for a full day of operation. And there are zero greenhouse gas emissions.

52. Exploring Mars

Space X Rendering of Mars Base Alpha

Elon Musk just tweeted this artist's rendering of his planned Mars Base Alpha. He plans to settle people on Mars in 2024. In 2023 he'll send a manned mission to explore Mars. In 2022, he plans on cargo missions to Mars. And in order to keep on schedule, he expects to start test launches of his Big Falcon Rocket (BFR) space ship in 2019. He just provided an update on BFR.

Interplanetary Travel

Musk showed off an updated version of the BFR. When it's finished he claims it's going to be the largest, most capable and most powerful launch vehicle ever built. Musk says it's an interplanetary transport system capable of going from Earth to anywhere in the solar system.

Lunar Mission with Tourists on Board

Musk also gave an update on the Space X trip to the moon. BFR will take off, have booster separation, go into orbit, fly around the moon and come back to earth in 4 or 5 days. Japanese billionaire Yusaku Maezawa and several artists will be onboard for their "moon vacation". Musk said there will be a number of test launches of the BFR before any people get onboard. The trip to the moon is planned for 2023.

REVIEW REQUEST

If you enjoyed reading this book and found it a good resource on innovation, I'd greatly appreciate your providing a review.

It's very easy to do. Go to the book's Amazon page. At the bottom of the page, you'll see a button that says "Write a customer review". Click that and you're all set.

Your review and support are very important and make a big difference to the author and their book's success.

Thank you.

Ed Kane

www.ingramcontent.com/pod-product-compliance
Lightning Source LLC
Chambersburg PA
CBHW030454220526
45464CB00006B/2535